THE FIRE THAT BURNS FOR THE LAST DAYS

The Fire That Burns for the Last Days

Copyright © 2019 Kevin S. O'Connor. All rights reserved.

No rights claimed for public domain material, all rights reserved. No parts of this publication may be reproduced, stored in any retrieval system, or transmitted in any form or by any means, electronic, mechanical, recording, or otherwise, without the prior written permission of the author. Violations may be subject to civil or criminal penalties.

Scripture taken from the New King James Version. Copyright © 1979, 1980, 1982 by Thomas Nelson, Inc. Used by permission. All rights reserved.

Scripture taken from the King James Version of the Bible.

ISBN: 978-1-63308-499-5 (paperback)
        978-1-63308-500-8 (ebook)

Interior and Cover Design by *R'tor John D. Maghuyop*

1028 S Bishop Avenue, Dept. 178
Rolla, MO 65401

Printed in United States of America

THE FIRE THAT BURNS FOR THE LAST DAYS

KEVIN S. O'CONNOR

CHALFANT ECKERT
PUBLISHING

TABLE OF CONTENTS

Dedication 1
Acknowledgments 3
Introduction 5

Chapter 1:   Sound Doctrine 7
Chapter 2:   Salvation Demands Change 13
Chapter 3:   The Fear of the Lord, Do We Fear HIM? 17
Chapter 4:   Call to Obedience, Faithfulness,
              and Devotion to God 23
Chapter 5:   It's Time to be Doers! 29
Chapter 6:   The Truth You Know 33
Chapter 7:   Nothing is Impossible 37
Chapter 8:   Take Up Your Cross; Being HIS Disciples 41
Chapter 9:   Let's Grow Up 45
Chapter 10:   There's NO Middle Ground with GOD 51
Chapter 11:   Walking In The Spirit 55
Chapter 12:   Wisdom From The Spirit 61
Chapter 13:   Power Through The Spirit 65
Chapter 14:   The Spirit is Already Here! 71
Chapter 15:   Stop Hiding Your Light 75
Chapter 16:   Distinguishing Holy From Unholy 79
Chapter 17:   How Does God See YOU? 83

Closing 87
About the Author 89

DEDICATION

I want to dedicate this book to my great grandmother, Ruby P. Niblack Bracken, who passed away before seeing the promises of the Lord come to pass in my life.

Also, my grandmother Deloris "Hannah" Miller for many years, was my refuge and mother in the faith. She knew from the moment I gave my life to Christ that He was going to use me in ministry.

ACKNOWLEDGMENTS

I want to acknowledge a few people who have made this book possible. I want to give all praise and glory to God, who was the true inspiration for this book.

I want to thank my wife, Carmen M. O'Connor, for standing beside me in ministry and for being an awesome woman of faith who always believed God had/has a destiny and purpose for our lives.

I want to thank my children Matthew, Tristen, Hadassah, and Rebekah for making Daddy want to be better at everything he does.

I also want to thank my mother, Denise A. O'Connor, who pointed me to Christ at a young age. I want to thank my twin brother, Briant, who has always been by my side, and my little sister, Charity, who never wavered in supporting me.

INTRODUCTION

There is a spiritual fire building and burning for a time such as this. It has been reserved for this generation and our particular issues.

As time grows shorter and shorter to the coming of our Lord, we as a church need to step out of the shadows of political and social correctness and stand up steadfast for truth and righteousness. We need to break free from what naysayers, agnostics, atheists, and a self-seeking world says. We need to start running bright, bold, and fearless with the Word, power, and love of God, as the world falls down around us. And never doubt it: The world is toppling swiftly!

The church needs to take a stand. We are supposed to be as bold as lions, but the majority of us are as helpless as kittens. All the while, our children have somehow wandered off the beaten path. All we do is say, "He seemed fine in church every week," or "She was an 'A' student," or "They never lacked anything; they were well provided for." I'm only going to deal with the church aspect because if that isn't right, the other two don't matter.

We need to stop assuming that just because someone attends church, it automatically makes them a part of God's Church. We don't need to learn how to play church; we need to receive Jesus Christ as our Lord and Savior! And after that, we, as a church, need to provide our children with godly role models, godly mentors, godly guidelines, and godly encouragement. Most of all, we need to show them a godly love and godly example!

The biggest problem with the church is that we spend too much time playing church and not enough time being the church.

CHAPTER 1

SOUND DOCTRINE

*I charge thee therefore before God,
and the Lord Jesus Christ, who shall judge the
quick and the dead at his appearing and his kingdom;
Preach the word; be instant in season, out of season;
reprove, rebuke, exhort with all long suffering and
doctrine. For the time will come when they will
not endure sound doctrine; but after their own
lusts shall they heap to themselves teachers, having
itching ears; And they shall turn away their ears
from the truth, and shall be turned unto fables.*

2 Timothy 4:1-4 (KJV)

This is very evident in this day and age: There is a turning away from sound doctrine. It's not the entire church, but it is a problem plaguing the church. Let's ask ourselves this question: What does *sound doctrine* mean? To answer that, let's define these two words from a biblical standpoint.

Doctrine is announcement and instruction. Doctrine, simply stated, is an announced instruction. *Sound* means entire, integrity, truth, without blemish, complete, full, perfect, sincere, without spot, undefiled, upright, and whole (*Strong's Hebrew Concordance*, 8549). Thus, sound doctrine means a truthful complete (or entire), perfect, undefiled announcement of instruction.

I believe it's time for the church to get back to sound doctrine and start living by the Word of God again. We need to stand as a Holy Church accepting the sinner, but not condoning the sin. So many churches have conformed to this world and its government, that they no longer know what sin looks like and are narrowing the definition of sin to limit what is called sin. Malachi 2:17 (KJV) says,

> *Ye have wearied the Lord with your words.*
> *Yet ye say, Wherein have we wearied him?*
> *When ye say, Every one that doeth evil is good*
> *in the sight of the Lord, and he delighteth in*
> *them; or, Where is the God of judgment?*

That is where a lot of the Church is, even though it goes totally against sound doctrine.

So, what is sound doctrine? Let's look at the definition one more time. Sound doctrine is a truthful, complete (or entire) perfect, undefiled announcement of instruction. What do we have as Christians that fits this definition? The Word of God; the Bible fits this definition perfectly. Many churches are afraid to preach the whole Bible; they are no longer preaching sound doctrine. Some twist the Word to fit their agenda; it sounds good, but it goes totally against the Word of God and sound doctrine. One prime example is the "gay movement" in churches today. A church that condones homosexual marriage is not following sound doctrine and is not of God period! That example fits the verse at the beginning of this chapter, *"For the time will come when they will not endure sound doctrine; but after their own lusts."* We are living in that day! A day of false teachers and prophets that Jesus spoke about in Matthew 7:15. He said that they are wolves in sheep's clothing. But He also said you shall know them by their fruit.

Sound doctrine will always bear good fruit, and those that preach false or unsound doctrine will bear bad fruit; thus, leading me into the purpose of sound doctrine.

Sound doctrine is a vital part of our faith. It's used to defend the faith, to refute naysayers, and to train Christians to live in such a way that the world would have no evil thing to say of the Church. The world needs to marvel at the life of a believer, not the sin of a believer.

> *Holding fast the faithful word as he hath been taught, that he may be able by sound doctrine both to exhort and to convince the gainsayers.*
> Titus 1:9 (KJV)

Paul was writing on how an elder must live, but you can see the purpose of sound doctrine.

> *Take heed unto thyself, and unto the doctrine; continue in them: for in doing this thou shalt both save thyself, and them that hear thee.*
> 1 Timothy 4:16 (KJV)

I love this verse because it challenges us as the Church. It challenges us to be holy; to watch ourselves in action and speech. That is the challenge I issue to the Church. Take heed unto thyself and the doctrine! Watch how you live and act, and make sure it agrees with the Word of God. Watch the doctrine you preach, ensuring it is in accordance with the Word because if you preach anything other than the Gospel presented in the Bible, there will be consequences. Paul said in Galatians,

> *But though we, or an angel from heaven, preach any other gospel unto you than that which we have preached unto you, let him be accursed. As we said before, so say I now again, if any man preach any other gospel unto you than that ye have received, let him be accursed.*
> Galatians 1:8 (KJV)

We need to warn those who preach false doctrine and bring them back to the truth to keep believers from following false teachings. We also need to set an example for the world so that they cannot speak evil of us. Paul wrote of this in Titus:

> *Young men likewise exhort to be sober minded. In all things shewing thyself a pattern of good works: in doctrine shewing uncorruptness, gravity, sincerity, Sound speech, that cannot be condemned; that he that is of the contrary part may be ashamed, having no evil thing to say of you.*
> Titus 2:6-8 (KJV)

We need, as a church, to get back to the Bible. We have allowed wolves to come in and preach trash from our pulpits, nay the Lord's pulpits! We wonder why the world is going to hell. It's because we let the world affect us, instead of us affecting the world. Thus some of the church is going to hell right along with them. We need to return to sound doctrine: doctrine that says homosexuality is a sin, racism is a sin, aborting is a sin, pornography is a sin, but God is willing to forgive you and save you! We need to scream to the world that you can't live whatever way you want and go to heaven. You must repent! Sometimes I wonder if we don't need to yell that at some churches. Some preachers are scared to say this, but I am not one of them. Salvation demands change!

So let's get back to sound doctrine, let's get back to the Bible! Let's start living for God again. Let us return to solid teaching. The Word of God is the pillar of our faith; let us return to it so that we can impact this world like never before. Let's not be conformed to this world; let's transform this world in Jesus Name! Amen! Praise the Lord!

CHAPTER 2

SALVATION DEMANDS CHANGE

*When Jesus had lifted up himself,
and saw none but the woman, he said unto her,
Woman, where are those thine accusers? hath
no man condemned thee? She said, No man,
Lord. And Jesus said unto her, Neither do
I condemn thee: go, and sin no more.*

John 8:10-11 (KJV)

In this verse, Jesus, after forgiving the woman, commands her to change her life. He says go and sin no more! In other words, go now and leave your life of sin. He puts a demand for change on her life. In this world of "greasy grace" or "cheap grace," the church has forgotten that although Salvation is free, it also demands change afterward. By cheap grace, I mean, salvation without the demand to change. Jesus didn't teach "cheap grace." Jesus said,

> *Because strait is the gate, and narrow is the way,*
> *which leadeth unto life, and few there be that find it.*
> Matthew 7:14 (KJV)

The Word of God is filled with teachings telling us to change our ways and to live Holy after Salvation. To love God and be saved, we must follow His commands. Why? God's Word says so. Jesus said, *"If anyone loves me, he will obey my teaching"* (John 14:23, NIV). He went on to say, *"He who does not love me will not obey my teaching."* (John 8:24, NIV). To love God is to follow His teachings!

I am not talking about salvation by works. I'm talking about obedience after salvation. Like the woman at the beginning of this chapter, after the Lord forgave her, He commanded her to leave her life of sin. We need to leave the sin in our lives and obey the Lord's teachings. We, as a church, need to look at what's going on all around us. "Greasy Grace" teaching is all around us.

There are churches telling homosexuals they don't have to change; they say that God accepts the way they live. That is false! God detests it! God accepts the sinner, not the sin! Further, God only accepts a sinner after he or she has been washed in Jesus' blood. After they have been forgiven, He demands they change their lifestyles!

> *Seek the Lord while he may be found;*
> *call on him while he is near. Let the wicked forsake*
> *their ways and the unrighteous their thoughts.*
> *Let them turn to the Lord, and he will have mercy*
> *on them, and to our God, for he will freely pardon.*
> Isaiah 55:6-7 (NIV)

God's Word tells us that Salvation demands change. If you claim to be saved, judgment starts with you! We the churches are the first to be judged. Peter says,

> *For it is time for judgment to begin with God's household; and if it begins with us, what will the outcome be for those who do not obey the gospel of God? And, "If it is hard for the righteous to be saved, what will become of the ungodly and the sinner?"*
> 1 Peter 4:17-18 (NIV)

This verse alone is enough to keep me following God and doing what is right. In John, it says:

> *This is how we know who the children of God are and who the children of the devil are: Anyone who does not do what is right is not God's child, nor is anyone who does not love their brother and sister.*
> 1 John 3:10 (NIV).

As much as people want to live their lives whatever way they want, you can't if you follow God, But the sad part is "greasy grace" teachers influenced by political correctness are still out there. They are out there condoning every kind of worldly sin and telling people that they don't have to change, they can live whatever way they want, and thousands of people who believe them are going to hell because they listen to a feel-good greasy grace gospel, rather than the truth. They are going to hell because they haven't heard the true Gospel. They are going to hell because they never got a chance to have a real committed relationship with the Lord Jesus Christ. A real relationship with God teaches you to say no to ungodliness and worldly passions and to live self-controlled, upright, and godly in this sinful world (paraphrased Titus 2:11-14).

It's a time for the church of Jesus Christ to start preaching the truth of God's Word. We need to shout it from the hilltops, and we need to say it as it is written:

> *Come back to your senses as you ought,*
> *and stop sinning; for there are some who are*
> *ignorant of God—I say this to your shame.*
> 1 Corinthians 15:34 (NIV)

We need to let them know God forgives and salvation is free, but both demand change. If we can get the church to start living right, the world will see us as we are supposed to be seen: as a city on a hill, lighting this world with the Gospel of Jesus Christ!

CHAPTER 3

THE FEAR OF THE LORD, DO WE FEAR HIM?

*And fear not them which kill the body,
but are not able to kill the soul: but rather fear him
which is able to destroy both soul and body in hell.*
Matthew 10:28 (KJV)

This verse speaks for itself, so I'll start with asking this question: Do you fear Him? Whose opinion matters most in your life: man's or God's? Who do you fear: man or God?

I see this as one of the biggest problems in this day and age: There is no fear of God. The world lives in sin; they've never feared God. But now some churches are following suit! Some churches now have no fear of God; instead, they seek after their own lust and opinion of men. They listen to the world rather than

God, and that is why homosexuality is running rampant in the church. The government is campaigning for gay rights; so, the church, controlled by political correctness to gain "social status," condones gay marriage and the homosexual lifestyle. They even ordain homosexuals to preach. God forbid this should go on any longer; they do not fear God. Woe to those churches, God will judge your sin!

Homosexuality is a sin, and God detests it, God judged sexual immorality, among other things, in Sodom and Gomorrah, and He intends to judge it and all other sin when Christ comes again. It is not only homosexuality that is running rampant, but sin in general, from the abortionists' butcher clinics to pornography on the internet, from murder at home to murder at the local school, from political scandals to church scandals! Why is sin running rampant? Because people have lost their fear of God! Some people say you should not fear Him, as in shaking and trembling, but I beg to differ. Yes! We must fear Him and respect Him and His statutes, everyone!

> *The fear of the Lord is the beginning of knowledge:*
> *but fools despise wisdom and instruction.*
> Proverbs 1:7 (KJV)

The Lord is saying that those who learn to fear Him have gained wisdom and knowledge. And that wisdom and knowledge start with a reverent fear of God. God is saying, "You have made a wise or right decision to fear me! But fools do not choose to fear me; only a fool despises my wisdom and instruction." Why is God saying, "Fear Me," to the world? He is saying this because a righteous God has to judge sin; a righteous God cannot stand for unrighteous sin. And God judges those who do evil or sin unless they repent and turn from their sinful ways!

> *Come, ye children, hearken unto me:*
> *I will teach you the fear of the Lord. What man is he that desireth life, and loveth many days, that he may see good? Keep thy tongue from evil, and thy lips from speaking guile. Depart from evil, and do good; seek peace, and pursue it. The eyes of the Lord are upon the righteous, and his ears are open unto their cry. The face of the Lord is against them that do evil, to cut off the remembrance of them from the earth.*
> Psalms 34:11-16 (KJV)

God not only stands to judge evil, but He is even going to wipe out the memory of evil and those who do evil! Unless they repent, God still judges those who do evil.

> *The fear of the Lord prolongeth days:*
> *but the years of the wicked shall be shortened.*
> Proverbs 10:27 (KJV)

America has become a country which has no fear of God, who lives by their own ideas and lusts.

> *Should you not fear me?" declares the Lord.*
> *"Should you not tremble in my presence?*
> *I made the sand a boundary for the sea,*
> *an everlasting barrier it cannot cross.*
> *The waves may roll, but they cannot prevail;*
> *they may roar, but they cannot cross it.*

But these people have stubborn and rebellious hearts;
they have turned aside and gone away.
They do not say to themselves,
'Let us fear the Lord our God,
who gives autumn and spring rains in season,
who assures us of the regular weeks of harvest.'
Your wrongdoings have kept these away;
your sins have deprived you of good.
"Among my people are the wicked
who lie in wait like men who snare birds
and like those who set traps to catch people.
Like cages full of birds,
their houses are full of deceit;
they have become rich and powerful
and have grown fat and sleek.
Their evil deeds have no limit;
they do not seek justice.
They do not promote the case of the fatherless;
they do not defend the just cause of the poor.
Jeremiah 5:22-31 (NIV)

Doesn't that sound like this country and fit some of the church in this present age? This country has no fear of God, or we wouldn't toss the Ten Commandments out of our public schools. This country has no fear of God, or they would not support homosexuals getting married! They would not support abortion clinics that murder babies in the womb. God doesn't see abortion as just stopping a pregnancy; He sees it as murder, plain and simple!

There are some in the church who have no fear of God; who shouldn't be in the church because they are not of the church. By not of the church, I mean not saved! If the fruit they bear is evil, they cannot possibly be a good tree. To fear the Lord is to hate evil. We know only the righteous or born-again person hates evil, but some in the church instead of hating sin, embrace it. Whether it is racism or homosexuality or abortion or pornography, some seem to embrace it. I can only say judgment is coming. Whether you believe me or not, it is coming anyway! We don't have to believe the Bible for it to be true. We don't have to trust in God for Him to do what He wills anyway.

He said in a loud voice, "Fear God and give him glory, because the hour of his judgment has come. Worship him who made the heavens, the earth, the sea and the springs of water."
Revelation 14:7 (NIV)

I charge thee therefore before God, and the Lord Jesus Christ, who shall judge the quick and the dead at his appearing and his kingdom;
2 Timothy 4:1 (KJV)

For he has set a day when he will judge the world with justice by the man he has appointed. He has given proof of this to everyone by raising him from the dead."
Acts 17:31 (NIV)

These verses are but a few that show us that God's judgment is coming! We need to ask this question of the fear of the Lord – Do we fear Him? It's not a question of if you'll bow, but when you will bow! Every knee shall bow, and every tongue will confess that Jesus Christ is Lord to the glory of God the Father. (Paraphrased Philippians 2:10-11 KJV)

FEAR GOD!

CHAPTER 4

CALL TO OBEDIENCE, FAITHFULNESS, AND DEVOTION TO GOD

*Therefore, with minds that are alert and fully sober,
set your hope on the grace to be brought to you
when Jesus Christ is revealed at his coming.
As obedient children, do not conform to the evil
desires you had when you lived in ignorance.
But just as he who called you is holy, so be holy in all
you do; for it is written: "Be holy, because I am holy."*
1 Peter 1:13-16 (NIV)

God has called us to live righteous, obedient, and holy lives and not to live sin-filled lives after salvation! We get saved out of the ignorance of this world, and into the knowledge of God and His Kingdom! We were brought out of being ignorant of God, into knowing and having a relationship with God through Jesus Christ. What this verse says is that now we are no longer ignorant of God but know Him; we must not live our old lives.

Let's look at this verse more closely. First, Peter says to "prepare your minds for action." Preparing your mind is the key to not conforming to this world or its desires. In Romans it says,

> *And be not conformed to this world:*
> *but be ye transformed by the renewing of your mind,*
> *that ye may prove what is that good,*
> *and acceptable, and perfect, will of God.*
> Romans 12:2 (KJV)

Now, after reading that verse, it is obvious that renewing our minds has something to do with not conforming to this world, but it really isn't clear how the renewing of the mind takes place. So now the question is: How does this renewing of the mind take place? Here is how Paul told the Ephesians to do it,

> *But ye have not so learned Christ;*
> *If so be that ye have heard him, and have been*
> *taught by him, as the truth is in Jesus:*
> *That ye put off concerning the former*
> *conversation the old man,*
> *which is corrupt according to the deceitful lusts;*

> *And be renewed in the spirit of your mind;*
> *And that ye put on the new man, which after God is*
> *created in righteousness and true holiness.*
> Ephesians 4:20-24 (KJV)

The renewing of your mind comes through the Spirit. Scripture says to be renewed in the spirit of your mind putting on the new man. We put on the new man through prayer and reading of the Word. We renew our minds the same way. Jesus said the Spirit would teach us all things. So, as we pray and read the Word, building our faith, our mind becomes like Christ. That is what Paul was talking about in 1 Corinthians 2. Paul talks about the Spirit of God teaching us, and in the end, Paul says this;

> *For who hath known the mind of the Lord,*
> *that he may instruct him? but we*
> *have the mind of Christ.*
> 1 Corinthians 2:16 (KJV)

So as we pray or commune with the Lord and read His word, through the Holy Spirit, our minds are renewed to that of Christ's!

Now, getting back to the verse at the beginning of this chapter, after you have "prepared your mind for action," being self-controlled and obedient children not conforming to your old desires is a lot easier to do. Now if we are called to be holy or obedient to God, why are so many "church folks" living for the devil? They profess Christ as Lord of their life but live like Satan rules it. Grace is not a license to sin. Paul said in Romans,

> *What then? shall we sin, because we are not under the law, but under grace? God forbid. Know ye not, that to whom ye yield yourselves servants to obey, his servants ye are to whom ye obey; whether of sin unto death, or of obedience unto righteousness?*
> Romans 6:15-16 (KJV)

We are to be slaves of righteousness; we are called to be obedient, faithful, and completely devoted to God. It is for our own good so that we may escape God's judgment on evil and disobedience. God will judge those who do not obey and believe in Him!

> *He will punish those who do not know God and do not obey the gospel of our Lord Jesus. They will be punished with everlasting destruction and shut out from the presence of the Lord and from the glory of his might.*
> 2 Thessalonians 1:8-9 (NIV)

The people in our churches that live like the devil need to wake up.

> *For I tell you that unless your righteousness surpasses that of the Pharisees and the teachers of the law, you will certainly not enter the kingdom of heaven.*
> Matthew 5:20 (NIV).

You can't live any way you want! God demands obedience, but in the society of immoral lifestyles, immoral acceptance, and political correctness, disobedience runs wild! Ours is not a Godly country; for the most part, America is not living for God. God will judge America for its disobedience and immorality.

*Like the nations the Lord destroyed before you,
so you will be destroyed for not
obeying the Lord your God.*
Deuteronomy 8:20 (NIV)

America, read that verse carefully because if you don't repent and come back to God, that is your fate. God will not put up with your immoral behavior forever. His day of judgment is coming, and only those who know God will be saved. So, seek the Lord while He is near. Shun evil, be obedient, and come back to God. Stop butchering unborn babies in your abortion clinics and stop promoting homosexuality; things like this plague our country, and it must stop. This is not just the secular world either. Church wake up, get disobedience and sin out. Get those pornography-obsessed preachers out from behind the pulpit and get them down at the altar. God is coming; you need to be ready. If you're not, you'll wish you had been. I am sure everyone in hell wishes they were ready when they died, but instead, they face an eternity of anguish obeying God is much more fulfilling!

CHAPTER 5

IT'S TIME TO BE DOERS!

But be ye doers of the word, and not hearers only, deceiving your own selves.

James 1:22 (KIV)

Another problem in the church today is that people hear God's Word but never do it, or act upon it. We've become hearers of God's Word only. Why did Jesus say those who only hear God's Word deceive themselves? The next chapter in James answers this question and more.

Yea, a man may say, Thou hast faith, and I have works: shew me thy faith without thy works, and I will shew thee my faith by my works.

James 2:18 (KJV)

Faith and works go together; they perfect each other, that's why it says in verse 17, *"Even so faith, if it hath not works, is dead, being alone."* James said that they deceived themselves because they thought they could have faith without action. If all you do is hear the Word, your faith is dead, because of the lack of action.

Let's look at the word *action*. Action is the process of doing or acting; an effect produced by something. Faith produces works and works perfect faith. Evidence for this is in James:

> *Was not Abraham our father justified by works, when he had offered Isaac his son upon the altar? Seest thou how faith wrought with his works, and by works was faith made perfect? And the scripture was fulfilled which saith, Abraham believed God, and it was imputed unto him for righteousness: and he was called the Friend of God. Ye see then how that by works a man is justified, and not by faith only.*
> James 2:21-24 (KJV)

Again, this is not salvation by works. Salvation is free! Works are just the product of your faith. But your faith is proven by what you do, thereby justifying your faith. Now, do you understand how works make faith perfect or complete your faith?

I think it is time for the church to get an alive faith that proved itself by doing what God said. We need to start being *Doers* of the Word, and we need to start obeying God. There is a difference between being justified in our own eyes and being justified in

God's eyes. That is how people deceive themselves; thinking they are justified by just hearing God. They have dead faith. You have to act on your faith for it to be justified. The church has gotten lazy. They are not willing to do what God said; they're not willing to act on what they believe, or what they're believing for. They believe, but that's as far as it goes.

> *Thou believest that there is one God; thou doest well: the devils also believe, and tremble.*
> James 2:19 (KJV)

That's what sets us apart from the world, not only do we believe, but along with faith, we put forth works and actions to completely perfect, prove, and justify our faith. Do you see why faith without works is dead?

So let's get moving. Just as we are set apart for God, our faith should be set apart from the world. Action brings our faith alive and purifies it. It's time to be doers!

CHAPTER 6

THE TRUTH YOU KNOW

*They claim to know God, but by
their actions they deny him.
They are detestable, disobedient and
unfit for doing anything good.*
Titus 1:16 (NIV)

*But mark this: There will be terrible times in the last
days. People will be lovers of themselves, lovers of money,
boastful, proud, abusive, disobedient to their parents,
ungrateful, unholy, without love, unforgiving, slanderous,
without self-control, brutal, not lovers of the good,
treacherous, rash, conceited, lovers of pleasure rather
than lovers of God—having a form of godliness but
denying its power. Have nothing to do with such people.*
2 Timothy 3:1-5 (NIV)

Some people and churches fit either the first or second verse or both of the verses above. The first verse says they claim to know God but deny Him by their actions. The second says lovers of pleasures rather than God, having a form of godliness but denying the power thereof. Now they don't know God or His power. They don't have a relationship with Christ. If they did, they would know him; they would also know and have the power of God in their life. They deny the Lord and His power. What power is Paul talking about? He is talking about the power of salvation and the power to change your disobedient ways and the miracle-working power of God. They don't want to give their old ways up to come to salvation. You have to give up control of your life to God. You have to confess Jesus as Lord. The word *LORD* means master, supreme, controller, master of, absolute ruler, eternal.

When you get saved, you're telling Jesus you want Him to be Lord of your life. You're saying you want Him to be in control. Some people want to stay in control of their lives; they deny the Lord and His power, they deny His Lordship and power, but still try to play church. Listen to me well; you can't play church and be saved. The only way to be saved is to have a relationship with Jesus Christ. You have to know the Lord and let Him rule and reign over and in your life. That's it – period. That's the truth, but we live in a generation who deny the truth.

> *They will turn their ears away from the truth and turn aside to myths.*
> 2 Timothy 4:4 (NIV)

That's the problem now: We've given up the truth. America has turned aside from the truth, turned from the only thing that will help; they've turned away from what will set them free!

> *"Then you will know the truth,*
> *and the truth will set you free."*
> John 8:32 (NIV)

It's not just the truth but the truth you know that sets you free. That's what we need to let America know. Come back to God; know the truth of God. Nothing else will set you free. Come back to the truth you have forsaken; without it, you have no hope. When we get set free, the power of God will be able to work through us for His purpose. I'll ask as Paul did in Galatians,

> *So again I ask, does God give you his Spirit and*
> *work miracles among you by the works of the*
> *law, or by your believing what you heard?*
> Galatians 3:5 (NIV)

It is because we believe; it's because of the truth you know. That is when obedience comes in. Let's come back to God. Let's believe and obey His Word. Let's get set free by the truth of His Word. Then, may the Lord work through us in power, so He will be able to pour out His Spirit on us in fullness for these Last Days.

CHAPTER 7

NOTHING IS IMPOSSIBLE

And Jesus said unto them, Because of your unbelief: for verily I say unto you, If ye have faith as a grain of mustard seed, ye shall say unto this mountain, Remove hence to yonder place; and it shall remove; and nothing shall be impossible unto you.
Matthew 17:20 (KJV)

In the last chapter, we reviewed how the truth you know sets you free, and how when we know that truth, and believe, God gives His miracle-working Spirit to us.

I want to shortly share how faith and through His Spirit nothing is impossible! Even when faith as small as a mustard seed. Nothing is impossible to those who believe.

> *Jesus said unto him, If thou canst believe,*
> *all things are possible to him that believeth.*
> Mark 9:23 (KJV)

If you know the story, you know the reason Jesus said, "If you can" was because the man said, "but if you can do anything help us." So, Jesus said, "If you can." Didn't you know everything is possible to him that believes? Jesus was saying to just have faith! Our faith is the trigger that gest God to act on our behalf. Why? Because faith pleases God, and without faith, it is impossible to please God.

> *And without faith it is impossible to please God,*
> *because anyone who comes to him must believe that he*
> *exists and that he rewards those who earnestly seek him.*
> Hebrews 11:6 (NIV)

We are human, and we have our limitations, but if we have faith that God can and will do what we ask Him because we're His children, nothing is impossible, because for us by ourselves all things are impossible, but with God nothing is impossible. Here is what Mark says:

> *Jesus looked at them and said, "*
> *With man this is impossible, but not with*
> *God; all things are possible with God."*
> Mark 10:27 (NIV)

Now the interesting thing is the word used here, the word *with*. We already know nothing is impossible for God, but Jesus said With God. Let's look at the meaning of this word *with*.

With - In the company of; near or alongside;
having, wearing or bearing; containing.

What Jesus was saying was that man by himself can do nothing, but for the man in the company of God, near or alongside God, having God, wearing or bearing God, or containing God nothing is impossible. Jesus said,

> *"I am the vine; you are the branches.*
> *If you remain in me and I in you, you will bear*
> *much fruit; apart from me you can do nothing.*
> John 15:5 (NIV)

So, with God, nothing is impossible for us.
I can do all this through him who gives me strength.
Philippians 4:13 (NIV)

Now the verse in Hebrews we read earlier in this chapter says that He rewards those who earnestly seek Him. We are told to earnestly seek God.

> *Beloved, when I gave all diligence to write unto you of*
> *the common salvation, it was needful for me to write*
> *unto you, and exhort you that ye should earnestly contend*
> *for the faith which was once delivered unto the saints.*
> Jude 3:3 (KJV)

I only brought up earnestly seeking God because, in the next few chapters, we'll be dealing with this topic in various ways. So many of the people in church are not earnestly seeking or following God.

CHAPTER 8

TAKE UP YOUR CROSS; BEING HIS DISCIPLES

*"Then Jesus said to his disciples,
if anyone would come after me, he must deny
himself and take up his cross and follow me."*
Matthew 16:24 (NIV)

This is a challenging verse. Why is it such a challenging verse? It's challenging because it tells us to live for God instead of ourselves. It means that we are to put aside selfish ambitions, the old sinful nature, and follow Christ. We are supposed to be imitators of Christ as dearly loved children. That means in action and speech. That's what the word *follow* means.

> *Follow* – To Proceed or come after; to
> pursue; to follow the course of;
> to obey; to come after in time or
> position; to ensure; to result;
> to attend to closely; to understand the meaning of.
> (*Strong's Bible Dictionary* says even to imitate.)

In just that one definition, there are many truths. There is something in that definition that will make you understand that verse in a new fullness. It shows you how serious Jesus was when He said it. We are to pursue Christ, to follow the course of Christ, to obey Christ, and to understand the meaning of Christ. We are to know who He is and what He is about; that's powerful.

Now the taking up of the cross is the crucifying of your old way of life or the old man–that old sin nature. When you give that old life up, you will find the new life Christ gives you.

> *For whoever wants to save their life will lose it,*
> *but whoever loses their life for me will find it.*
> Matthew 16:25 (NIV)

Luke says to do this daily. We are not to do it just on Sunday, not just on holidays, not just when we're in a valley of trouble, but we are to take up the cross and follow Him daily. But the Church has gotten lazy. Why has the church gotten lazy? It's because of the fear of persecution. When we start living the Christian lifestyle, persecution will come. Paul gave this charge to Timothy, "*In fact, everyone who wants to live a godly life in Christ Jesus will be persecuted.*" (2 Timothy 3:12, NIV)

The church needs to figure out that persecution will come, and get over it. If they persecuted Jesus, they'll persecute us. We need to endure those sufferings as Christ did no matter what. That way, this verse will be complete; *"If we live, we live to the Lord; and if we die, we die to the Lord. So, whether we live or die, we belong to the Lord"* (Romans 14:8, NIV). Let's follow Christ with all of our heart. Jesus said those who don't take up their cross and follow Him are not worthy of Him and cannot be His disciples. That is in Matthew 10:38 and also Luke 14:27.

We need to learn to take up our cross and follow Christ because if we don't, we cannot be His disciples. That is what the church needs. We need a "Cross Carrying Revival." We need a reawakening to carry our cross and follow Christ in these last days!

CHAPTER 9

LET'S GROW UP

*Like newborn babies, crave pure spiritual milk,
so that by it you may grow up in your salvation,
now that you have tasted that the Lord is good.*

1 Peter 2:2-3 (NIV)

This is a problem for some Christians; it's a problem for them to grow up. So many Christians today don't want to grow up, or some don't know how to grow up. I'll say this as plainly as possible, "Church, Lets Grow Up!" In Jesus Name, Let's Grow Up.

Many of you are properly asking how to grow up? I will tell you; not because I am so smart, but because God's Word said so. It's because God is so smart, Amen?

Peter 2:2 says to *"…crave pure spiritual milk, so that by it you may grow up in your salvation."* It's by that pure spiritual milk that you grow up in your salvation. Now, what is that pure spiritual milk?

It's the Word of God. In the King James Version, that verse says, *"...desire the sincere milk of the word that you may grow thereby."*

Now for milk to do you any good you have to drink it. That is what you are to do when you read the Bible. You are to drink the Word into your spirit. Now that doesn't mean to just read it. It means to believe it when you read it. It says to crave or desire that spiritual milk. When you desire or long for something, you won't spend much time longing for something that does supply the object of the longing. So, you believe this thing you're longing for can supply or fulfill that need or longing in your life. When you crave pure spiritual milk, the pure spiritual milk of the Word, you've got to believe that it is going to supply your spirit with nutrients to make you grow up in your salvation. Now, what does supply mean?

Supply – To complete, to contribute, to aid, to fill, to make complete, to furnish fully.

Supplying the Word helps us to grow up in our salvation. This growing up is reaching maturity. When something or someone grows up, it becomes mature. Maturity is grown or built. Here is what it says in Ephesians:

So Christ himself gave the apostles, the prophets, the evangelists, the pastors and teachers, to equip his people for works of service, so that the body of Christ may be built up until we all reach unity in the faith and in the knowledge of the Son of God and become mature, attaining to the whole measure of the fullness of Christ.
Ephesians 4:11-13 (NIV)

In these verses, we see that we are to be built up to maturity. The phrase "built up" means to rear up, to establish, to construct, to arrange, to edify, and what we're building up to is maturity. So, when it says to build up, it's saying to rear up, establish, construct, arrange, and edify until mature.

> To rear up until mature;
> To establish until mature;
> To construct until mature;
> To arrange until mature;
> To edify until mature!

Later in this chapter, it talks about growing up into Him who is the head, which is Christ. We see a phrase that coincides with the subject of "grow up," which means to reach maturity or to reach adulthood.

When you mature, you can attain the whole measure of Christ. Some of your religious people may say, "You cannot attain the whole measure of Christ on earth." Oh Really? Then why does it say in the next verse…?

> *Then we will no longer be infants, tossed back and forth by the waves, and blown here and there by every wind of teaching and by the cunning and craftiness of people in their deceitful scheming.*
> Ephesians 4:14 (NIV)

Now you say we cannot reach the whole measure of the fullness of Christ on earth. We know no one will be blown here and there by every wind of doctrine or by the cunning and craftiness of men in Heaven. None of this goes on in Heaven; it happens on the earth, in the nasty here and now. So, we become mature, attaining to the whole measure of the fullness of Christ on earth to protect us from being blown around by every wind of teaching and the cunning and craftiness of men.

I am not saying we obtain perfection on earth, only maturity. I want to make that clear, but we can reach maturity, and we need to reach maturity attaining to the whole measure of the fullness of Christ. In other words, let's grow up so we will stop thinking like children. *Brothers and sisters, stop thinking like children.*

> *In regard to evil be infants,*
> *but in your thinking be adults.*
> 1 Corinthians 14:20 (NIV)

Infants are sinless, and adults think wisely, Praise be to God! This also coincides with earnestly seeking God, because to crave God's Word is to crave God, and if you crave something, you will earnestly seek it. In fact, the word *crave* in the Greek means just that.

> *Crave* – involves the idea of urgent need;
> strictly a demand for something due;
> implies a search for something hidden.

It is so wonderful to know how to grow up in Christ; how to earnestly seek Him. How much could we as a church do if we all just grew up and earnestly sought God? If we would stop feasting and playing and start fasting and praying, God would help us. God would work in us, and through us. God would reveal

His glory and power to His people if only we would stop seeking this world and start seeking God – if we would start earnestly contending for the faith.

Let's stop being just mild-mannered Christians, living meager lives among this world, never stepping into the supernatural power of God that could transform us if we would only let Him. But let's grow up into our salvation; attain that whole measure of the fullness of Christ that can transform us from meager to mighty; that power that makes us the head and not the tail. That power that transforms us from a victim to a Victor! Grow up, grow up, and grow up in the Name of Jesus, Amen!

CHAPTER 10

THERE'S NO MIDDLE GROUND WITH GOD

*"No one can serve two masters.
Either you will hate the one and love the other,
or you will be devoted to the one and despise the
other. You cannot serve both God and money.*
Matthew 6:24 (NIV)

*"Whoever is not with me is against me,
and whoever does not gather with me scatters.*
Matthew 12:30 (NIV)

I am about to make a lot of New Age people mad. There is NO middle ground with God. There are a lot of people who say, "I'm not with God or against God." Well, you have to be one or the other. There is no neutral, and there is no middle ground with God. You can't serve God and the world. If you say you do, you are lukewarm and are in danger of God's destruction. Don't take my word for it; lets see what the Bible says.

> *So, because you are lukewarm—neither hot nor cold—I am about to spit you out of my mouth.*
> Revelations 3:16 (NIV)

The days of mediocre Christianity are coming to an end. God is tired of lukewarm Christians living with one foot in the Kingdom and one foot in the world. He is tired of Christians trying to serve Him and the world. There is no neutral position with God. You are either for Him or against Him, not both! The reason people are lukewarm is simply that they don't want to give up their old lives completely. If they got on fire for God, they would have to step into the light of God and that old sinful nature would be exposed. Jesus said it this way in John,

> *This is the verdict: Light has come into the world, but people loved darkness instead of light because their deeds were evil. Everyone who does evil hates the light, and will not come into the light for fear that their deeds will be exposed. But whoever lives by the truth comes into the light, so that it may be seen plainly that what they have done has been done in the sight of God.*
> John 3:19-21 (NIV)

Why do we have mediocre Christianity? Why are there lukewarm Christians? It's because they don't want to step into the light! They are afraid to step into the light of God's righteousness because they're not living for Him totally. They say they live by the truth, but if they were to step into the light, their lies would be exposed.

The time has come for us to start living by the truth; it's time for us to get on fire for God. It's time to realize there is no middle ground with God. He said He wished that we were either hot or cold, but not both. Jesus said you're either for me or against me; you can't serve God and the world. The Bible teaches us not to love the world or anything in it because the world and its desires will pass away, but those who do the will of God will live forever (paraphrased 1 John 2:15-17).

Some of you ask, "Well, how do we walk in the Light?" In 1 John 2, He tells us how to do this. I'll give you three verses that jumped out at me, and then you can read the whole chapter.

> *We know that we have come to know him if we keep his commands.*
> 1 John 2:3 (NIV)

> *Whoever claims to live in him must live as Jesus did.*
> 1 John 2:6 (NIV)

> *"Anyone who claims to be in the light but hates a brother or sister is still in the darkness."*
> 1 John 2:9 (NIV)

The second verse leaves little room for error because if you walk like Jesus did, you will not be lukewarm or mediocre in your walk; you will be on fire and in the Light. You'll want to serve and obey God, and you will love your brother if you walk as Jesus did. It's that simple. You either walk as Jesus did or you don't. You're either for Him or against Him; there is NO middle ground with God.

CHAPTER 11

WALKING IN THE SPIRIT

For as many as are led by the spirit of God, they are the sons of God.
Romans 8:14 (KJV)

This I say then, walk in the Spirit, and ye shall not fulfil the lust of the flesh.
Galatians 5:16 (KJV)

If we live in the Spirit, let us also walk in the Spirit.
Galatians 5:25 (KJV)

In the last chapter, we talked about there being no middle ground with God, and we saw that we are to talk as Jesus walked. Now we all know that Jesus was led by the Spirit, and if we walk like Jesus did, we must live and walk in the Spirit. The very fact that Jesus lived a sinless life shows He walked in the Spirit. The Bible says He offered Himself spotless before God through the Holy Spirit.

> *How much more shall the blood of Christ, who through the eternal Spirit offered himself without spot to God, purge your conscience from dead works to serve the living God?*
> Hebrews 9:14 (KJV)

In the verse at the beginning of this chapter, it says that if we walk in the Spirit, we will not fulfill the desires of the flesh. That is because the Spirit desires things contrary to the sinful nature (see Galatians 5:17), so by this to walk as Jesus walked is to walk in the Spirit.

Walking in the Spirit is more than just having the Holy Spirit in you; it's about being in step or in sync with what the Spirit desires to do in you and through you.

> *Those who live according to the flesh have their minds set on what the flesh desires; but those who live in accordance with the Spirit have their minds set on what the Spirit desires.*
> Romans 8:5 (NIV)

> *Whether you turn to the right or to the left, your ears will hear a voice behind you, saying, "This is the way; walk in it."*
> Isaiah 30:21 (NIV)

The Holy Spirit leads us into the things the Lord would have us to do. A lot of people hear the Spirit say, "Here is the way," but they never walk to it. Walking in the Spirit is keeping in step or in sync with what the Spirit desires for you to do. The key is not only hearing what He wants you to do but to walk in it after He tells you which way to take.

It's time for the church to start walking in the Spirit. If you don't walk in the Spirit, you're not going to walk in God's power! The Holy Spirit is the power of God for us. The miracle-working anointing is in the Holy Spirit. Let me give you two examples of men who walked in the Spirit. Peter was walking in the Spirit when his shadow was healing people. Paul lived and walked in the Spirit because he only went to towns where the Spirit led him; he walked in the Spirit so much that the rags he used, when they touched other people, healed them instantly.

Its time for us to walk in the Spirit! Its time for us to walk in step with the Spirit. *"God is spirit, and his worshipers must worship in the Spirit and in truth."* John 4:24 (NIV). It does not say they have a choice to worship in Spirit and in truth; it says they must worship in Spirit and in truth because the Spirit and the truth both set you free. Jesus was telling us that to touch heaven and receive from God, it must be done through the Spirit. It is only by the Spirit that our lives are transformed. That is why it is so important for us to learn to walk in the Spirit. That is why we need to be sensitive to the Holy Spirit. Scripture says,

> *Now the Lord is that Spirit: and where the Spirit of the Lord is, there is liberty. But we all, with open face beholding as in a glass the glory of the Lord, are changed into the same image from glory to glory, even as by the Spirit of the Lord.*
> 2 Corinthians 3:17-18 (KJV)

It is the Spirit that transforms lives and brings the power and anointing of God. The Holy Spirit brings the fire of God's presence!

> *But ye shall receive power, after that the Holy Ghost is come upon you: and ye shall be witnesses unto me both in Jerusalem, and in all Judaea, and in Samaria, and unto the uttermost part of the earth.*
> Acts 1:8 (KJV)

The Holy Spirit brings the power of God. The Holy Spirit is the power of God; the power of God in the Bible is described as fire. John the Baptist said this speaking to Jesus in Matthew,

> *"I baptize you with water for repentance. But after me comes one who is more powerful than I, whose sandals I am not worthy to carry. He will baptize you with the Holy Spirit and fire."*
> Matthew 3:11 (NIV)

So, let's learn to walk in the Spirit. When we do the power and anointing and fire that comes with Him will transform us and empower us to accomplish His will for our lives.

One last quick verse and statement for this chapter:

> *And I will put my Spirit in you and move you to follow my decrees and be careful to keep my laws.*
> Ezekiel 36:27 (NIV)

God gives us the Holy Spirit to empower us to be able to obey Him through the Spirit. We are incapable of not sinning, but the

Holy Spirit gives us the power to follow His commands, and He gives us the Power to say no to sin.

The Holy Spirit is the fire that burns for the last days. It will either refine and transform you into what God desires or it will consume you because you were not ready and chose to live in disobedience and sin unwilling to change. We'll talk about that in the next few chapters. Remember a Son of God is led by the Spirit of God.

CHAPTER 12

WISDOM FROM THE SPIRIT

Now Stephen, a man full of God's grace and power, performed great wonders and signs among the people. Opposition arose, however, from members of the Synagogue of the Freedmen (as it was called)—Jews of Cyrene and Alexandria as well as the provinces of Cilicia and Asia—who began to argue with Stephen. But they could not stand up against the wisdom the Spirit gave him as he spoke.

Acts 6:8-10 (NIV)

In the last chapter, we talked about walking in the Spirit; now I want to discuss how wisdom is from the Spirit. This Wisdom comes from God through the Holy Spirit. Let's look at the verse above. It says they could not stand up against his wisdom, or the Spirit, by whom he spoke because he was walking in the wisdom of God, not the wisdom of men. Notice it says "the Spirit by whom he spoke." Stephen was walking in the Spirit and the wisdom he was speaking with, which came from the Spirit.

Paul, speaking of God's wisdom, said,

> *These are the things God has revealed to us by his Spirit. The Spirit searches all things, even the deep things of God. For who knows a person's thoughts except their own spirit within them? In the same way no one knows the thoughts of God except the Spirit of God.*
> 1 Corinthians 2:10-11 (NIV)

This is the wisdom Stephen had through the Spirit. The only way to receive from God is through the Holy Spirit; whether it is wisdom from God or the anointing of God or deliverance. Whatever the case may be, it is revealed through the Holy Spirit. Here is what Jesus said in John,

> *But when he, the Spirit of truth, comes, he will guide you into all the truth. He will not speak on his own; he will speak only what he hears, and he will tell you what is yet to come. He will glorify me because it is from me that he will receive what he will make known to you. All that belongs to the Father is mine. That is why I said the Spirit will receive from me what he will make known to you."*
> John 16:13-15 (NIV)

Now the main purpose of receiving wisdom from God is to know Him better. It is written,

> *I keep asking that the God of our Lord Jesus Christ,
> the glorious Father, may give you the Spirit of wisdom
> and revelation, so that you may know him better.*
> Ephesians 1:17 (NIV)

The Lord not only wants us to know Him more, But He also wants us to know His power and the inheritance we have in Him. We, as a church, need to start walking in the wisdom of God. All we have to do is ask God to reveal His wisdom to us, but we have to be humble and submitted to God. We have to be ready to live by His wisdom, and willing to change if we have been living in a way contrary to that wisdom.

The Bible is the wisdom of God, spoken by the Holy Spirit, revealed to man. God wants to reveal His wisdom and Word to us through His Spirit. He also wants to reveal His power to us; He wants us to know our inheritance in Him. God has given us His power through the Holy Spirit. Think of what kind of impact we would have if all the church walked in the wisdom and power of God that comes from walking in the Spirit. Let's move past our fleshly selves and look to God, and be the Church He has called us to be; the one that the gates of hell cannot stand against. The verse at the beginning of this chapter said, *"Now Stephen a man full of God's grace and power did great wonders and miraculous signs among the people."* Not until we start walking in the Spirit will we receive this power.

CHAPTER 13

POWER THROUGH THE SPIRIT

But ye shall receive power, after that the Holy Ghost is come upon you: and ye shall be witnesses unto me both in Jerusalem, and in all Judaea, and in Samaria, and unto the uttermost part of the earth.
Acts 1:8 (KJV)

And, behold, I send the promise of my Father upon you: but tarry ye in the city of Jerusalem, until ye be endued with power from on high.
Luke 24:49 (KJV)

God has given us power and authority on the earth through the Holy Spirit. But so many churches don't know the power of God in their lives, or they don't know how to walk in that power after they get it.

For the last few chapters, we've been talking about walking in the Spirit. To receive the power that comes through the Spirit, you have to walk in the Spirit. Walking in the Spirit is being able to discern those things of the Spirit.

> *The person without the Spirit does not accept the things that come from the Spirit of God but considers them foolishness, and cannot understand them because they are discerned only through the Spirit.*
> 1 Corinthians 2:14 (NIV)

It is the Holy Spirit that reveals the things of the Spirit to us. He gives us spiritual discernment. In 1 Corinthians 2:16, Paul describes the spiritual discernment we receive as *putting on the mind of Christ*.

The Spirit gives us discernment in order to receive from the Lord. In the last chapter, we have seen how the Holy Spirit takes from what is Christ's and gives it to us. Now we see that He gives us discernment to receive it.

So, to stay in step with the Holy Spirit and the power, anointing, and wisdom He brings, we've got to keep our spiritual ears of discernment opened! We have received power and authority in Jesus through the Holy Spirit. You may ask, a many have, what power do we have? All of Heavens! Jesus said, *"Then said Jesus to them again, Peace be unto you: as my Father hath sent me, even so send I you."* (John 20:21, KJV)

How did the Father send Jesus? IN POWER! Everything Jesus did we can and must do. Jesus said in John 14:12 that we would not only do what He did but that we would do greater things because He went to the Father! Now I'll say it again: We have power through the Spirit!

It's time for us to start walking like we have that Power! Let's stop talking about walking in it, let's do it! The power of the Holy Ghost is the fire that burns for the last days. The Holy Ghost is about to rain the fire of God's power down like never before on this earth. Fire either refines or destroys. What will happen to you?

Religion or Relationship?

> *I indeed baptize you with water unto repentance; but he that cometh after me is mightier than I, whose shoes I am not worthy to bear: he shall baptize you with the Holy Ghost, and with fire:*
> Matthew 3:11 (KJV)

> *And, behold, I send the promise of my Father upon you: but tarry ye in the city of Jerusalem, until ye be endued with power from on high.*
> Luke 24:49 (KJV)

> *But ye shall receive power, after that the Holy Ghost is come upon you: and ye shall be witnesses unto me both in Jerusalem, and in all Judaea, and in Samaria, and unto the uttermost part of the earth.*
> Acts 1:8 (KJV)

I started with these verses in the last chapter, I know, but they are relevant in this chapter as well. In the last few chapters we've been talking about the Holy Spirit, and how to walk in the Spirit, – how to walk in the wisdom, power, and authority He brings us. It is because the Holy Spirit is the fire that burns for the last days. It is He that brings us from just a religion, into a relationship with God. He brings us from form to function.

In the end, the ones that get turned away are the ones Jesus never knew. Jesus said: *"Then I will tell them plainly, 'I never knew you. Away from me, you evildoers!'"* (Matthew 7:23, NIV).

How do we know Christ? The Spirit testifies of Him, and through the Spirit, Christ lives in us.

> *I have been crucified with Christ and I no longer live, but Christ lives in me. The life I now live in the body, I live by faith in the Son of God, who loved me and gave himself for me.*
> Galatians 2:20 (NIV)

> Paul said, *I pray that out of his glorious riches he may strengthen you with power through his Spirit in your inner being, so that Christ may dwell in your hearts through faith. And I pray that you, being rooted and established in love, may have power, together with all the Lord's holy people, to grasp how wide and long and high and deep is the love of Christ, and to know this love that surpasses knowledge—that you may be filled to the measure of all the fullness of God.*
> Ephesians 3:16-19 (NIV)

> Jesus said, *And I will ask the Father, and he will give you another advocate to help you and be with you forever—the Spirit of truth. The world cannot accept him, because it neither sees him nor knows him. But you know him, for he lives with you and will be in you.*
> John 14:16-17 (NIV)

> *On that day you will realize that I am in my Father, and you are in me, and I am in you.*
> John 14:20 (NIV)

I am going to stop here for a moment. We see that Christ lives in us through the Spirit. The Spirit comes to bring us into a relationship with God, so that we may know the Lord, and He gives us His Spirit to empower us to obey Him. That is the difference between a religion and a relationship. Religion is just a form of godliness that has no power. That power is the Holy Spirit. You don't know God by religion, but by a relationship through the Spirit. Christianity is not a religion but a relationship with Christ through the power of the Holy Spirit because the Spirit takes from what is Christ's and gives it to us. He reveals Christ to us.

It's time for the church to step out of religion and into a relationship with Christ. There are many self-proclaimed Christians walking around with a powerless religion, having no idea what a relationship with Christ is all about. It's time to get the power of God in our lives again. I speak of the fire and power of God that comes through the Holy Spirit to bring us into a relationship with God so we may know God. Anyone who knows God will obey Him.

Jesus said,

Ye are my friends, if ye do whatever I command you.
John 15:14 (KJV)

Do you see the importance of walking in the Spirit? When you receive the Holy Spirit, you come into right relationship with God, but to have a lasting relationship, you must keep in contact. That is what walking in the Spirit is, just as you have to keep in contact with a person on earth to know them and to be called their friend. So, it is with God, and the Holy Spirit is our way to keep in contact with God. We move from just a religion to a relationship, through the fire and power of the Holy Spirit.

CHAPTER 14

THE SPIRIT IS ALREADY HERE!

*And when the day of Pentecost was fully come,
they were all with one accord in one place.
And suddenly there came a sound from heaven as of a
rushing mighty wind, and it filled all the house where
they were sitting. And there appeared unto them cloven
tongues like as of fire, and it sat upon each of them.
And they were all filled with the Holy Ghost,
and began to speak with other tongues, as the Spirit gave
them utterance. And there were dwelling at Jerusalem
Jews, devout men, out of every nation under heaven.*
Acts 2:1-5 (KJV)

What do these Scriptures mean? Simply put, the Holy Spirit was poured out on all flesh. People are always talking about when God pours out His Spirit in the last days; they say it like they are waiting for it to happen. They talk about the prophecy in Joel as if it hadn't happened yet, but the Lord did it on the day of Pentecost. Peter said, "But this is that which was spoken by the prophet Joel." (Acts 2:16 KJV) Peter goes on to quest the prophecy in Joel 2:28-32. It started on the day of Pentecost, and you can see throughout the book of Acts how God continued to pour out His Spirit on all who believed.

"While Peter yet spoke these words, the Holy Ghost fell on all them which heard the word." (Acts 10:44, KJV) Then Peter went back to Jerusalem and told the story of what happened. *"As I began to speak, the Holy Spirit came on them as he had come on us at the beginning."* (Acts 11:15, NIV) These people not only received the Holy Spirit, but they received it in the same way with the same intensity as Peter and the others did on the day of Pentecost! Praise God.

This is probably one of, or maybe the most important chapters of this book. The Spirit is already here.

I hear this phrase all the time: *When God pours out His Spirit in the last days*. It has been the last days for the last two thousand year. Where have you been? God sent His Spirit on the day of Pentecost, and He hasn't gone anywhere. Jesus said,

> *And I will pray the Father, and he shall give you another Comforter, that he may abide with you for ever;*
> John 14:16 (KJV)

The reason I said this is the most important chapter is because people say revival will come when God pours out His Spirit in the last days, but the Spirit is already here. Stop waiting for what is already here, stop waiting for the Spirit, and start walking in the

Spirit. The Spirit was poured out; He is just waiting for us to step into His flow. He has been moving since the day of Pentecost; the Lord is waiting for you to step into what He is doing.

People keep saying revival is coming when God pours out His Spirit on all flesh. The Spirit has already been poured out. Now for a moment, let's look at this word *revival*. What is revival? You know sometimes we confuse it with healings or miracles. Revival in the most literal Christian sense is simply a renewed zeal to obey God.

Let's review quickly. God's Spirit is here already, and people say revival is coming when this happens. If God's Spirit has already come, revival has come with Him.

Why are we not seeing it? That is what these last few chapters focus on–walking in the Spirit. You can have the Spirit and not know how to walk with Him. Revival comes through the Spirit as you walk in him, and He teaches you to be more like Christ. Then you will have a renewed zeal to obey God.

It is time for the church to stop waiting for the Spirit and start walking in the Spirit. I heard one pastor say, "Stop praying for power and start praying with power." Stop waiting for the Spirit to move; He's already moving–get into the flow. The Holy Spirit is our guide. If you're not walking with Him, He can't show you where to go or which path to take. True revival will come when we start walking in the Spirit and when the church realizes that God has already given us the keys to the Kingdom and that God already sent His Spirit to teach us how to use those keys.

Wake up Church – The Spirit is ALREADY HERE!

CHAPTER 15

STOP HIDING YOUR LIGHT

"Or suppose a woman has ten silver coins and loses one. Does she not light a lamp, sweep the house and search carefully until she finds it?"
Luke 15:8 (NIV)

*"You are the light of the world.
A town built on a hill cannot be hidden.
Neither do people light a lamp and put it under a bowl.
Instead they put it on its stand, and it gives light to
everyone in the house. In the same way,
let your light shine before others, that they may see
your good deeds and glorify your Father in heaven.*
Matthew 5:14-16 (NIV)

You know in these days of casual or mediocre Christians, this may be the biggest problem: We hide our light. We don't stand out in the world. We either let our light shine or try to shine so brightly that we fool ourselves into thinking we are super Christians, particularly at church (though as soon as we step out of church, the light gets covered again). Or, we become the king of saints that shine at home, among family, with that which is familiar, and we lose sight of what is important to God. Notice throughout this book I have been using the term mediocre Christianity. When something is mediocre, it doesn't stand out. It's just the norm. Let's look at the definition of mediocre for a moment.

Mediocre – Common; fair; undistinguished

This definition, unfortunately, rings true to much of the Body of Christ. To be mediocre is to be common, fair, or undistinguished. To be undistinguished is to be unnoticeable. In other words, your light can't possibly shine to its fullest potential if you are second-rate, common-place, monotonous, and lackluster. Who would want to aspire to a God whose people are all jaded? No one! They have that in the world.

The world does not notice mediocre Christians; we need to make ourselves known to the world. We need to distinguish ourselves! We need to stand out; they need to be able to see that we have something different, something they want or need. We need to be exceptional or well above average to draw the world's attention, or to get them to notice what God has for them. We need to move from being mediocre to being radical Christians. Let's look at the definition of radical for a moment.

> *Radical* – Drastic; making extreme changes in views, conditions, or habits; carrying convictions or theories to their fullest applications.

Radical Christians will act drastically to get people saved or to witness to people. A mediocre Christian will give an average effort to the things of God, but a radical Christian gives it there all, they give a maximum effort. It is time to take the bowl off your candle and let your light shine to the max. Let's make a difference; let's be the difference–stop hiding your light.

At the beginning of this chapter, the woman was radical about finding that coin. Now let's look at that parable of the lost coin in its fullness.

> *"Or suppose a woman has ten silver coins and loses one. Doesn't she light a lamp, sweep the house and search carefully until she finds it? And when she finds it, she calls her friends and neighbors together and says, 'Rejoice with me; I have found my lost coin.' In the same way, I tell you, there is rejoicing in the presence of the angels of God over one sinner who repents."*
> Luke 15:8-10 (NIV)

Just like the woman who was looking for the lost coin, it is our job as a church to seek the lost for God. Jesus came to seek and to save those who are lost. Should we, as His servants, do any differently?

The woman was radical about looking for that coin, and the Word says that she swept the house and searched carefully until she found it. She was pretty radical about finding that coin. Let's examine the first thing she did. She lit her lamp. Why? So she could see. If she had not lit her lamp, she wouldn't have been able to see where she was going, and she wouldn't have been able to see the coin when she came to it.

Now we see how when we let our light shine, how it not only lets the world see us, but it lights up the world so we can find the lost. When you let your light shine, you can see the floor to sweep it and find the coin or the lost souls, with your lamp lit, you can see where you're going. A lot of the church is running around with a bowl over its light, or some don't even have their lamp lit. If we want something to happen, let your light shine.

What is the light you might ask?

For you were once darkness, but now you are light in the Lord. Live as children of light (for the fruit of the light consists in all goodness, righteousness and truth)
Ephesians 5:8-9 (NIV)

So, the light I am talking about is the light of God's salvation that was placed in you when you were born again. Remember, in Matthew 5:16 at the beginning of this chapter, which said to let your light shine before men so they could see your good deeds and praise your father in heaven? So, doing good or living right is a way of letting that light shine, and when you let your light shine, you can and will draw those who are lost.

So, STOP hiding YOUR Light!

CHAPTER 16

DISTINGUISHING HOLY FROM UNHOLY

*Her priests do violence to my law and profane
my holy things; they do not distinguish between
the holy and the common; they teach that there is
no difference between the unclean and the clean;
and they shut their eyes to the keeping of my
Sabbaths, so that I am profaned among them.*
Ezekiel 22:26 (NIV)

This is true in many churches today. You can't tell the difference between them and the world. I mentioned this a few times throughout the book, but this is a very critical subject. This is a very important subject to the Lord because God hates it when we don't distinguish between holy and unholy. God has punished nations for this. That does not exclude God's people, because, in the verse above, he is talking about Israel. It was the priests doing these things, and it's still the priest's profaning God by not distinguishing between the holy and the common.

In this generation of hypocritical Christianity, we have not painted a good picture of ourselves to the world. Because we say we are different, sanctified, set apart doesn't amount to much. The question is: Are we who we say we are? The world can't tell. And why? For one, we don't act any different than the world. W don't make a distinction between saved and unsaved. If you are born again, you are different. Rather you should be different. In the last chapter, we talked about radical and mediocre Christianity. Mediocre meant common, and radical was distinguished, tanding out or uncommon, drastic – just the opposite of mediocre. Look at the verse at the beginning of this chapter. How did the priests profane the Lord? They did not distinguish between the holy and the common. It says there was no difference between the unclean and the clean. We know now Holy is clean, so common must be unclean. We know common is mediocre, so holy must be Radical.

Many didn't distinguish between the holy and the common, but that was not the only thing that profaned God. The Bible says they taught that there was no difference between the two. Churches are doing this very thing today. They profane God by teaching that homosexual marriage is okay. By handing out condoms, they teach that fornication is okay. By condoning abortion, they teach that murder is okay. NO! None of these things are okay! All of these acts are sins, and if the people don't repent, turn from them, and seek God, they will take them to hell.

The people who teach these things are no better than hypocrites, maybe even worse. At least a hypocrite teaches what is right. He just doesn't practice what he preaches. These people teach to do evil. They teach there is no right or wrong; a feel-good doctrine that is sweeping America and taking it by storm. "If it feels good, do it, then it must be right" is the mentality. It's the same mentality that caused judgment to fall on Sodom and Gomorrah, and it's the same mentality that is going to cause God's judgment to come upon the earth in the end. It's not truth as you perceive it to be; God's truth is perfect, complete, without restraint, unconditional, and sovereign.

So, what sets us apart? How are we sanctified? How are we different? Jesus said:

> *Sanctify them by the truth. Your word is truth.*
> John 17:17 (NIV)

It is the truth that Jesus has set you free and sanctified you. Only when you know this does it become the distinguished fact between the holy and the common. When you know that Jesus paid the price for your being set apart and you know that He has freed you, then you can apply it to your life, and start using that truth to distinguish first of all in your own life; the holy and the unholy, and then in the world around you.

In the equation of distinguishing holy from common, clean from unclean, and radical from mediocre, Jesus is the distinguishing factor. Jesus is what sets us apart from the world, so we need to act like it. Make the distinction and stand out. The Jesus in me and the Jesus in you could be the distinguishing factor that set someone else free and sanctifies them into the family of God! Can they see Him in you? Can they see the difference in you? Make sure they can!

CHAPTER 17

HOW DOES GOD SEE YOU?

Then said Jesus to those Jews which believed on him, If ye continue in my word, then are ye my disciples indeed; And ye shall know the truth, and the truth shall make you free.

John 8:31-32 (KJV)

Jesus answered them, Verily, verily, I say unto you, Whosoever committeth sin is the servant of sin. And the servant abideth not in the house for ever: but the Son abideth ever.

John 8:34-35 (KJV)

Out of the sixteen chapters that came before this one, I pray that you would take hold of this one. I was challenged and forced to do a lot of growing while writing this chapter. Nothing in this book is as valuable as what

I share here. Are you ready to be challenged to a whole new level in God? If so, let's get started. Look at the first two verses at the beginning of this chapter:

> *Then said Jesus to those Jews which believed on him, If ye continue in my word, then are ye my disciples indeed; And ye shall know the truth, and the truth shall make you free.*
> John 8:31-32 (KJV)

First, notice that the Bible says He spoke to those Jews which believed on Him. Then He says if you continue in my Word, then ye are my disciples indeed. Because there is a common, feel-good doctrine in the church today that says, "If you just believe in Christ, you are His disciple!" Many people just assume by believing in Christ they are His disciples, but Jesus says these words "IF" and "THEN."

Right after the "if" and "then" He says, *"And ye shall know the truth, and the truth shall make you free."* How will we learn this truth that will set us free? The answer to that question is found in John 8:31. We continue in His Word. When we continue in His Word, we become His disciples indeed and learn the truth that sets us free.

Two more questions arise, and the answers will set you free and take you to a new level in God you've never known before. The first one is: What is the Truth we need to know? The second is: What do we need to be set free from?

No doubt judging by what they said to Jesus, these questions were on the minds of those Jews who were talking to Jesus. Read what it says,

> *They answered him, We be Abraham's seed,*
> *and were never in bondage to any man:*
> *how sayest thou, Ye shall be made free?*
> John 8:33 (KJV)

So, I'll ask these questions again: What truth did they need to know and what did they need to be set free from? Jesus gave them the answer to these questions very clearly in verses 34-36. Let's start with verse 34, *"Jesus answered them, Verily, verily, I say unto you; whosoever committeth sin is a servant of sin."* (John 8:34, KJV) Wow! We have already answered one of the questions. What did they need set free from? They needed set free from sin, but let's go on and tie it together.

> *And the servant abideth not in the house for ever:*
> *but the Son abideth ever. If the Son therefore*
> *shall make you free, ye shall be free indeed.*
> John 8:35-36 (KJV)

Jesus says if you commit sin that you are a servant to sin, and the servant abideth not in the house forever: but the Son abides forever. One more verse before we tie this together.

> *Nevertheless what saith the scripture?*
> *Cast out the bondwoman and her son: for the son*
> *of the bondwoman shall not be heir with the son*

> *of the freewoman. So then, brethren, we are not children of the bondwoman, but of the free.*
> Galatians 4:30-31 (KJV)
> Referencing Genesis 21:10-12

What we, like those Jews, needed was to be set free from sin, because if we are a servant of sin, we cannot be an heir with the son. If we stay servants of sin, we are like the son of the bondwoman. We will be cast out or cut off from being heirs. So, what Jesus said was that the servant of sin could not stay in His Father's house, neither can he be an heir with Christ, But He said the Son abideth ever. What son? The son of the freewoman! How do we become sons and daughters of the freewoman? Let's read John 8:36 one more time: *"If the Son therefore shall make you free, ye shall be free indeed."*

What was the truth that would set those Jews free? What is the truth that will set us free? We need to know the Son, Jesus, has set us free from sin and made us sons and heirs with Him in the Kingdom of God. We must know who we are in God. Who are we in God? Who are you to God? Does He see you as His son, or are you still a servant to sin? I know I am not the first preacher to preach this, but the Lord gave me a word and said, "Remind my people who they are!" The fire that burns for the last days is when God's people realize who they are afresh, and start living and being who and what God called them to be!

How does God see YOU?

CLOSING

As time closes in on us, humanity and hell are breaking loose on earth. It is becoming more evident that the church needs to be who we claim to be. Never have we been more needed. Never have the fields been so ripe for harvest. Souls are crying out for an answer. They are looking for truth and love. They are seeking comfort. Where are the churches that have been commissioned to be a light to the Gentiles, the unsaved, and the hopeless? Where are the ambassadors of Christ? Who will stand up for what should be?

The goal of writing this book was not to point out faults but to open the eyes of us as believers to start being the Church of the Living God, whom the gates of hell cannot prevail against. We need to stop walking in mediocrity and begin walking a powerful living walk with the Lord Jesus Christ!

I pray with all sincerity that this book was of value to you, that it built a fire in you for God that can never be extinguished. I pray that it opened your eyes to the necessity of living for God and walking upright before God in these last days. I pray that it inspired you to go deeper in God than you have ever gone, and farther in Him than you've ever been. That is the essence of this book, to inspire you to go for more in God, to stir a hunger for God in you again.

Wake your spiritual eyes and ears to see and hear what God is saying and doing. He will do what He wants to do through you if you will seek Him. The fire that burns for the last days ignites when God's people get hungry enough to go all the way with Him. The only thing that matters is pleasing Him and living for Him.

When we decrease, He increases.

ABOUT THE AUTHOR

Pastor Kevin S. O'Connor resides in Coffeyville, Kansas with his wife Carmen, and their children. Pastoring *Agape Fellowship Church*, which was established in the living room of their home and is continuously expanding and assistance the community and those in need.

Agape' Fellowship Church

Pastor Kevin S. O'Connor

WEBSITE:
https://agapefc17.wixsite.com/agapefellowship

FACEBOOK:
https://www.facebook.com/AgapeFC17/

EMAIL:
afc.ck17@gmail.com

Note from the Publisher

Are you a first time author?

Not sure how to proceed to get your book published?
Want to keep all your rights and all your royalties?
Want it to look as good as a Top 10 publisher?
Need help with editing, layout, cover design?
Want it out there selling in 90 days or less?

Visit our website for some exciting new options!

www.chalfant-eckert-publishing.com

www.ingramcontent.com/pod-product-compliance
Lightning Source LLC
Chambersburg PA
CBHW070241090526
44586CB00035B/1376